Sounds

By the end of this book you will know more about:

- How sound is made.
- How sound travels.
- Pitch and loudness.
- Different instruments.

You will:

- Use Fact Files, books, the Internet and CD-ROMs to help you answer questions.
- Carry out tests.
- Record results in tables.

Task
1

How sounds are made

We live in a world full of sound. You notice it every time you go for a walk. You hear the roar of traffic, the rustle of leaves, a friend calling you, or music playing through an open window.

How does this happen?
These children have some ideas.

Sounds are all around us

* Are they right? How do you think sounds reach our ears? Draw or write to show your ideas.

* How do you think sounds are made?

Making an alarm call

Class 6 are going on a mountain walk with their teacher, Mr Hill.

"We might need to call for help," said Mr Hill. "Is shouting good enough? Or should we take something that makes a loud noise?"

Read the children's ideas.

✴ What do you think? Draw or write to show which method you think would be best for calling for help. Explain why. Think about:

• How can you find out which sound would be heard at the greatest distance?

• How can you find out if the sound would be heard in every direction?

• Which sound would get the attention of rescuers?

Calling for Help!

If you get into difficulties or become lost, use the international signal for distress to raise the alarm.

1 Six blasts on a whistle or six shouts, six torch flashes or six waves.

2 Pause for one minute.

3 Repeat.

The pause is important. You need to listen for an answering signal of three whistle blasts, shouts or torch flashes.

Task 3 Lots of ears!

- Look at these animals. What do you know about their ears?

- Use books, CD-ROMs and the Internet to find the answers.

Why do rabbits keep turning their big, sound-collecting ears?

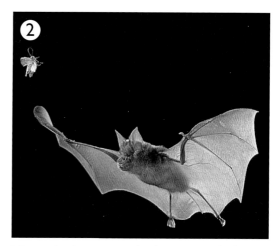

How do bats use their ears to help them catch insects?

How does an elephant use its huge ears to keep cool?

How do we know a song thrush must have ears?

Why do the ears of a fox point forward as sound detectors?

Frogs have ears on the side of their heads. What can they hear in the water?

Sounds are made when objects or materials vibrate.

Task 4

How to see tiny vibrations

All these things make sounds.

They make a sound when they **vibrate** – when they quiver or shake very quickly.

Washing machine shaking

Throat vibrating

Cat purring

you need:
- table tennis ball
- bowl of water
- tuning fork

There are ways of seeing tiny vibrations.

⚡ Strike a tuning fork on the table. Hold the vibrating fork in front of a bright light. Can you see the tips vibrate?

⚡ Tape or glue a table tennis ball to a thread. Hold it up. Gently rest the side of the vibrating fork against the ball. What happens?

⚡ Dip a vibrating fork into a bowl of water. What happens?

⚡ Can you explain what is happening? Show your ideas by drawing and writing.

⚠️ *Don't look directly at bright lights.*

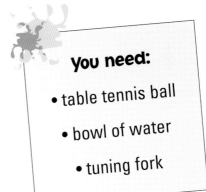

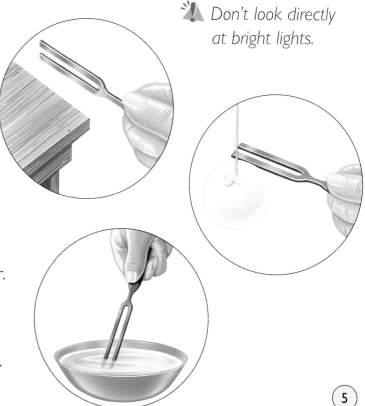

Task 5

More about tuning forks

How can you tell how much different tuning forks are vibrating?

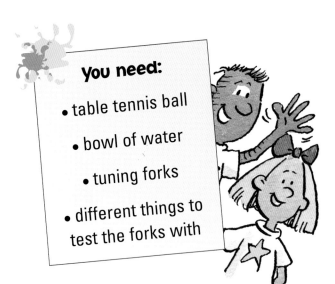

you need:
- table tennis ball
- bowl of water
- tuning forks
- different things to test the forks with

✦ Test different sizes of tuning forks. You could test them against a table tennis ball, or in a bowl of water.

● What will you observe or measure?

● What must you keep the same?

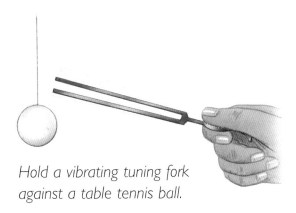

Hold a vibrating tuning fork against a table tennis ball.

Put a vibrating tuning fork in water

✦ Copy the table and record what you see.

Size of tuning fork	How I tested it	What I observed or measured

Words to learn and use:
quiver
sound waves
tuning fork
vibrate

✦ Complete Task Sheet 1.

you need:
- drum
- drumstick or beater
- rice

Task 6

Beat that drum!

✦ You can't see a drum skin vibrate. But try scattering some rice on the drum skin. Beat the drum and watch what happens.

✦ Hold up the drum, with rice on the top drum skin. Beat the bottom drum skin. What happens? Why?

⭐ Sound vibrations can travel through different materials.

What can you hear?

✦ Look at the pictures. How are the sounds heard?

✦ Show your ideas by drawing and writing.

1 What can they hear?

3 What can she hear?

5 What could you hear?

6 What could you hear now?

4 What can she hear now?

2 What can they hear now?

Sounds through materials

It's hard to believe but sound travels better – and faster – through solids like walls and doors than it does through the air.

So, if someone is shouting in the room next door, why is the shouting quieter when you close the door? Well, the sound has to travel through air before it reaches the solid door. Then it travels through the door and through air again before reaching your ear.

The better the connection between the sound maker and the solid object, the better the sound travels. The better the connection between the solid object and your ear, the better you hear the sound. So, if you put your ear to the door when someone is banging it you will hear the sounds much more loudly.

Sound also travels well through liquids. You might not be able to hear the whistle in the swimming pool when you are under water, but you would hear a sound made in the water – like a hammer banged on the pool floor.

Sounds through string
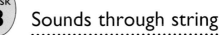

You can feel a tuning fork vibrate although you can only hear a very quiet sound. The sound is travelling through the air to your ears. Tie the fork in the middle of a piece of string. Hold the ends of the string against one of your ears – but not in it!

✦ Strike the fork against a table edge. Listen closely. What do you hear? Does sound travel better through air or through string?

✦ Try other metal objects on the string, such as a kitchen fork, a spoon or a wire rack.

★ How to identify the types of materials through which sound travels.

Task 9 String telephones

✦ Read what these children said about making a string telephone.

Making the holes for a string telephone can be dangerous. You may need an adult's help.

We tied our string to a paper-clip. That stopped it slipping through the hole.

You have to whisper. Some people shouted. You could hear them without the telephone.

We found how to send a message round a corner. You have to keep the string from touching the wall.

We experimented to find the best string telephone.

✦ Draw and write down your own ideas about making a string telephone. You could use a computer to help you.

Look at these pictures showing you how to make a string telephone and then make your own.

What makes a clearer telephone – is it the pots you use, the string, or the length of the string? How will you judge which is the clearest telephone?

Complete Task Sheet 2.

you need:

- string
- small plastic pots

⭐ Some materials can prevent sound reaching your ears.

Your ears are important

Your hearing is precious. When you prevent your ears working properly, you put yourself in danger.

Wearing your hood up can stop you hearing traffic. When your hood is up, you should look around extra carefully.

If you work in a noisy place, you need ear protectors to stop your ears being damaged. There are strict rules about wearing ear protectors. They should cover your ears completely and fit well on your head. How are these six people breaking the rules?

✴ Which materials would make good ear protectors?

✴ Be a sound buster! Make a leaflet, a poster or a short play about the dangers of loud noises to your ears.

Task 12 Silencing sound

✦ Find something that makes a sound. Put it in a box. Then try wrapping it in different materials. Try cloth, newspaper and bubble wrap. Can you still hear it?

✦ Which materials absorb the sound and make it quieter? Write why you think that is.

Task 13 A carpet in the library

✦ Read what the children of Class 5 said about their school library.

✦ Why do you think the library was quieter after a carpet and curtains were put in? Draw and write down your ideas.

You couldn't work in our library. There was too much noise.

Our Head teacher bought a carpet. She put up curtains.

There are no echoes. It's really quiet.

You could hear every chair scrape. Even people whispering sounded loud.

Now the library is really quiet. It's easier to concentrate.

Fact File

Unsafe sounds

Schoolboy may have died while listening to CD player

A schoolboy, who cycled into the path of a car and was killed, may have been listening to a personal CD player.

Malcolm Green (13) had been warned never to use the CD player when cycling, an inquest was told. Several witnesses said that Malcolm did not appear to hear the car. "The earpiece of the CD player was in the boy's ears and the play button was on," said PC Mervyn Brown. The coroner recorded a verdict of accidental death.

Compare how well different materials muffle sound.

Scientific Enquiry
Investigating sound control

Some materials muffle or stop sound travelling. These materials are called sound **insulators**.

You work for Soundbusters Ltd. A fax arrives asking you to test which material is the best sound insulator.

✦ Which material do you think will be the best sound insulator? Make a prediction.

✦ Plan your test. How will you make it fair? How will you record your results?

✦ You could use a sound sensor to measure the sound.

✦ Write a fax to Soundbusters Ltd to show your results. Say how your results matched your prediction.

✦ Complete Task Sheet 3.

you need:

• two small boxes that fit one inside the other

• a transistor radio that fits into the smaller box, or a home-made buzzer circuit

• materials that might muffle sound

• sound sensor (if you have one)

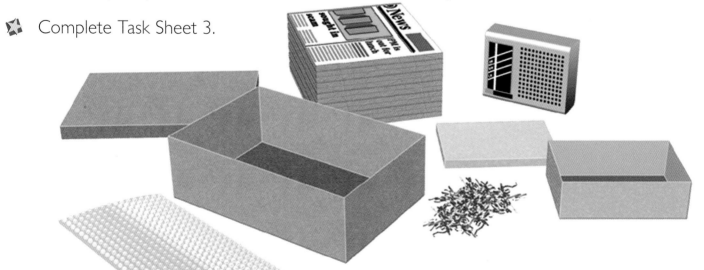

Pitch describes how high or low a sound is.

Twanging rulers

When you twang a ruler, you move the air around it.

 Hold the ruler upright against a cupboard door or a table edge. Then twang it.

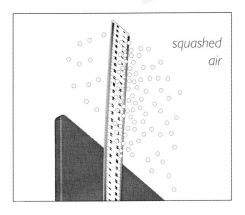
squashed air

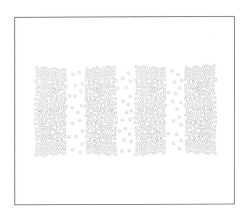
squashed air

1 As the ruler moves one way, it squashes the air together on one side and thins the air on the other.

2 As the ruler moves the other way, it squashes the air on the other side.

3 As the ruler bends back and forth, it squashes the air first on one side, then on the other. Tiny particles of air are pressing on their neighbours like people pushing each other in a crowd. This is how sound is made.

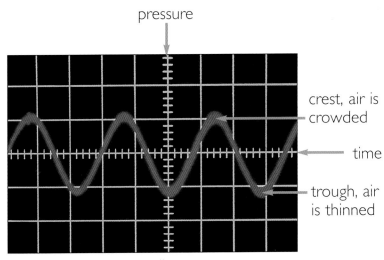

pressure

crest, air is crowded

time

trough, air is thinned

Sound waves on an oscilloscope

The sound moves out from the ruler through the air. These movements are called **waves**. Sound waves can be observed on an **oscilloscope**.
The **crest** of a wave is where the air is squashed. The **trough** of the wave is where the air is thinned.

Extra Challenge

 Use a slinky spring to model how sound moves through air.

 Hang the slinky from your hand. Let a few coils go from your fingers. Draw what you see.

 Look for CD-ROMs and web sites that show how sound moves through the air.

Scientific Enquiry
Different tuning forks

Hold a tuning fork loosely between your finger and thumb. Strike it on a firm surface such as a table.

Now make the sound louder by holding the base of the vibrating fork against a table top.

Compare several different tuning forks and record your data on Task Sheet 4.

How do their sounds vary?

We call how high or low a sound is, its **pitch**.

Wave shapes

When we draw sound waves in books we draw them to look like curves. We do this because this is what sound waves look like when they are observed on an oscilloscope. These pictures show how different types of sounds are drawn.

Loudness

You can change the loudness of a sound:

- A loud sound, like a shout, makes tall waves.

- A soft sound, like a whisper, makes low waves.

Pitch

Pitch is how high or low a sound is.

- A bat's squeak is very high. The waves are packed together.

- A loudspeaker hum is very low or deep. The waves are long.

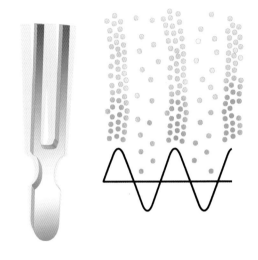

Shout

Whisper

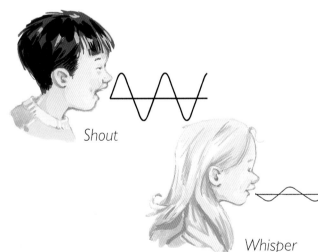

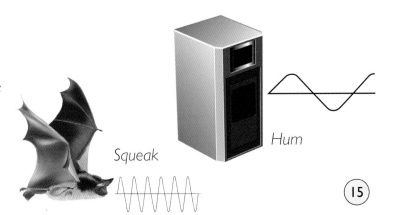

Squeak

Hum

How loud are these?

✨ Which of these are loud sounds?
Which are soft sounds?

✨ Can a sound be loud and high? Can a sound be loud and low?

A whisper

Talking

Rustling leaves

Thunderclap

Aircraft taking off

Pneumatic drill

How to change the pitch and loudness of drum sounds.

Task 18

Making a loud noise

5

- Press your hands together hard. You may be pressing hard, but there is no sound.

- Now clap using only your fingers. How much noise do you make?

- Clap with your whole hands. You are squashing the air between your hands and making a loud noise.

- Look at the table. Think of some other ways of making a loud noise.

- Complete Task Sheet 5.

Loud noise	Force used	Size of the maker	Vibrating material
Drum beat	Hitting with a beater	Large drum	Plastic drum skin

How to make a loud noise

If you want to make a loud noise, you can:

- hit very hard. A large **force** makes the drum louder.

- use something **big**. A large drum makes more noise than a small one when hit the same way.

- choose the right **material**. Steel guitar strings are louder than nylon ones when plucked the same way.

- keep the material tight or taut. A taut drum skin or guitar string can make a louder noise than a loose one.

When a noise is made louder, we say that it is **amplified**.

Words to learn and use:
amplify
crest
force
insulate
oscilloscope
pitch
soundproof
trough
volume
waves

⭐ How to change the pitch and loudness of stringed instruments.

Task 19   Make a box guitar

✸ Make a guitar like this one with elastic band strings.

✸ Twang the strings.

✸ Make changes so that you can play a high note, a low note and one between the two.

You have changed the pitch of the note.

✸ How many ways can you change the pitch?

you need:

• tissue box

• different sizes and thicknesses of elastic bands

• pencil as a bridge

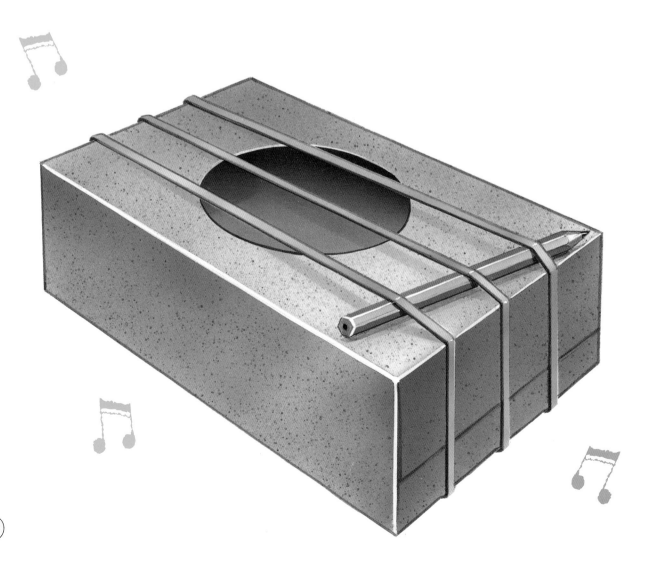

Scientific Enquiry
Investigating pitch

▶ 6

✦ Investigate the pitch of your box guitar. How does changing parts of the instrument affect the pitch of a note?

✦ You could change:

- the thickness of a string

- the length of a string

- the tightness of a string.

  Try to keep the **loudness** of the note the same.

✦ Predict what will happen before you make the change.

✦ Copy and complete this table.

What I changed	What I predicted	What I observed

✦ Copy and complete these two sentences:

> To make a note higher, you should…
>
> To make a note lower, you should…

✦ Complete Task Sheet 6.

Sounds can be made by air vibrating.
Predict how to change the pitch of a sound made
by air vibrating.

 Task 21 Bottle flutes

7

Adding water to a bottle changes the amount of air in it.

- Put a bottle on the table and hold it steady. Rest your lower lip on the edge of the bottle opening and blow. The bottle will make a hooting sound. The sound is made by the air vibrating inside the bottle.

- How could you change the pitch of the sound?

- Now try blowing across bottles of different sizes. What do you notice about the size of the bottle and the pitch of the note? Write one sentence that links the size of the bottle and the pitch of the note.

- Use several bottles of the same size. Pour different amounts of water in each one so each one has a different amount of air in it. Blow across the bottles. Write one sentence that links the amount of air in the bottle to the pitch of the note.

- Complete Task Sheet 7.

 you need:

- clean, empty glass bottles, some in different sizes and some in the same size

- water

 Take extra care with glass bottles.

⭐ Altering the length of the air column changes the pitch of wind instruments.

Task 22

Scientific Enquiry
Making a kazoo

you need:
- thin card tube
- greaseproof paper
- elastic band

✦ Make a kazoo from a kitchen roll tube and a piece of greaseproof paper.

✦ Hum into it. Notice how it buzzes.

✦ Change the pitch of the buzz. Try using longer and shorter tubes.

✦ Make a table to show your results.

Length of tube	My prediction	Type of buzz

✦ Copy and complete this sentence:

The longer the tube…

HUM...
HUM...

HUM...
HUM...

Fact File

Exploring wind instruments

Wind instruments make a note when you blow through them as the air inside vibrates. A short kazoo has a higher pitch than a long kazoo because the amount of air vibrating in the tube is less than in a long kazoo. The length of vibrating air in woodwind instruments is called the **air column**. The length of the air column in many woodwind instruments can be altered by covering the fingerholes with fingers or keys. This makes sounds of different pitches.

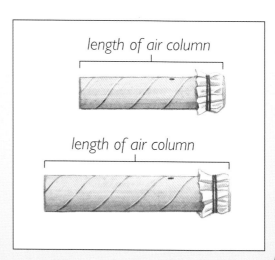

length of air column

length of air column

Checkpoint 1

Different types of instruments

✦ Here are some musical instruments from all around the world. Look at each musical instrument.

✦ Write about all the ways you could:

- change its pitch

- change its loudness.

The skins on this African drum are pulled tight with the laces.

This is a tambour. The player hits the stretched skin with a hand or a drum stick.

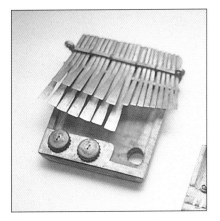

This is a thumb piano. You make sounds by twanging the metal strips.

This harp has strings of many different lengths.

The player blows across these South American pan pipes.

This is an Australian digeridoo. The player's lips vibrate as it is played.

Musical instruments

⚜ Look at this picture of children practising music.

- How are they making sound?

- What is vibrating for the guitarist?

- What are the blankets for? How will they work?

Summary

Which of these do you know and which can you do?

- I know that sounds are made when objects or materials vibrate.
- I know that sound vibrations can travel through different materials.
- I know how to identify the types of materials through which sound travels.
- I know that some materials can prevent sound reaching your ears.
- I can compare how well different materials muffle sound.
- I know that pitch describes how high or low a sound is.
- I know how to change the pitch and loudness of drum sounds.
- I know how to change the pitch and loudness of stringed instruments.
- I know that sounds can be made by air vibrating.
- I can predict how to change the pitch of a sound made by air vibrating.
- I know that altering the length of the air column changes the pitch of wind instruments.

Complete your **Science Log** to show how well you know these and how well you can do them.
Circle a face for each statement.